Blended Families

Yours, Mine and Ours

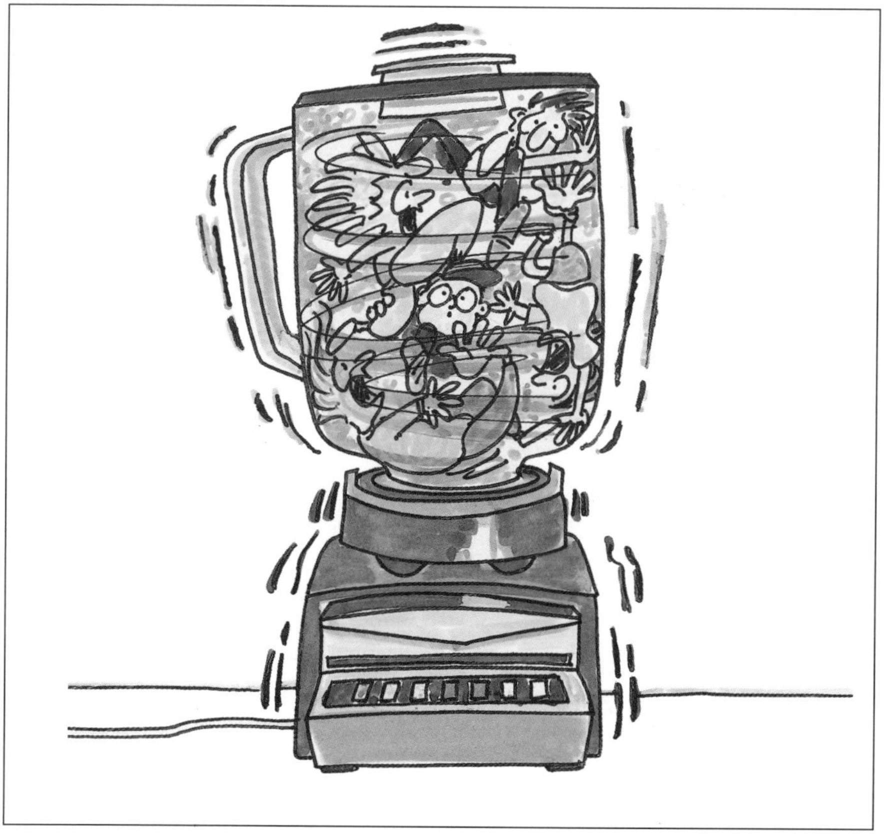

Serendipity House / P.O. Box 1012 / Littleton, CO 80160

TOLL FREE 1-800-525-9563 / www.serendipityhouse.com

© 1989, 1999, 2000 Serendipity House. All rights reserved.

00 01 02 03 04 / **FN series•CHG** / 7 6 5 4 3 2 1

PROJECT ENGINEERS
Lyman Coleman
Mike Shepherd

WRITING TEAM
Richard Peace, William Cutler, Andrew Sloan, Cathy Tardif

CARTOONS
Robert Schull

PRODUCTION TEAM
Christopher Werner, Sharon Penington, Erika Tiepel
The Serendipity Staff

ACKNOWLEDGMENTS

To Zondervan Bible Publishers
for permission to use
the NIV text, and Bible study notes
The Holy Bible, New International Bible Society.
© 1973, 1978, 1984 by International Bible Society.
Used by permission of Zondervan Bible Publishers.

Questions and Answers

1. **What is unique about this course?** The combination of three activities in one integrated program:
   ❒ Learning about the issue
   ❒ Interacting in small groups
   ❒ Studying the Bible

2. **Who is it for?**
   ❒ Home Bible Study groups
   ❒ Sunday school and other church groups
   ❒ Community organizations

3. **Where and how can I use this program?**
   ❒ Classrooms with movable chairs
   ❒ One-day seminars
   ❒ Weekend retreats
   ❒ Courses from seven to thirteen weeks

4. **How long is each session?** 90 minutes

5. **What if I do not have 90 minutes?** Divide sessions 1-6 into two sessions, making the course thirteen weeks instead of seven.

6. **How much does the course leader have to know about the subject?** Very little. This book provides all of the material. The leader convenes the meeting, makes introductory remarks, and follows the agenda.

7. **What about the group interaction?** This is directed by a Handout which each person is given at the beginning of the session. The Handout needs to be photocopied for every member. Another option is to provide each group member with his or her own course book (see page 5 for a detailed agenda to follow for each session).

8. **Why do you divide into subgroups of 4 to 6?** To allow everyone to share.

9. **How would you go about dividing the group?** Divide the number of participants in the group by 4 to 6 to determine the number of subgroups needed. Then, ask the group to count off—1, 2, 3, etc.

10. **Would you have the same groups meet every session?** That is up to you. There are advantages both ways.

11. **How does this course fit into the larger educational structures of the church?** This is an entry-level, short-term group for people with special needs or specific interests.

12. **Can this group continue as an ongoing small group after this course is over?** Yes. In the last session, the group is encouraged to make a contract or covenant to stay together and move on to the Growth Stage of a small group. A full description of the ongoing 201 Study courses are described inside the back cover.

13. **Are there other felt need courses available?** Yes, see page 61 for a complete list. For other curriculum for small groups, please call Serendipity at 1-800-525-9563.

CHECKLIST BEFORE THE SESSION

❒ ROOM ARRANGEMENT: Movable chairs for subdividing into groups of 4 to 6.

❒ HANDOUTS: Every person needs a Handout or the course book for every session. Permission is given for you to photocopy the Handout. Remember, there are two sides to the Handout. You may also want to photocopy the Caring Time part of the session as well.

❒ SPLIT SESSIONS: If you want to divide a session because you do not have 90 minutes, there is an Ice-Breaker to kick off the second part which you will need to photocopy from this book and give to the group.

❒ BIBLES: The Bible passage for discussion has been included in the Handout. However, if you want the group to read from their own Bibles, ask the people in the group to bring their Bibles.

❒ COURSE BOOK: Be sure to bring the book to the session and follow the agenda for each part of the session.

Agenda for Each Session

15 Minutes

ICE-BREAKER / Groups of 4 to 6
Divide the group into subgroups of 4 to 6 for a few minutes to get acquainted. Give the Handout—Side One to everyone.

You have permission to photocopy the Handout (both sides) for the session as needed, or you may prefer to provide each group member with his or her own course book.

5 Minutes

INTRODUCTION TO THE ISSUE / All Together
Bring the subgroups back together to listen to the introductory remarks for the session.

20 Minutes

DISCUSS THE ISSUE / Groups of 4 to 6
Regather in groups of 4 to 6 (same groups) to answer the questions on the Handout (Side One).

20 Minutes

BIBLE STUDY / Same Groups of 4 to 6
Stay in the same subgroups of 4 to 6 to discuss the Bible Study questions found on Side Two of the Handout.

Option 1: If you have a full 90 minutes for a session, follow the three-part agenda.

Option 2: If you only have 60 minutes for the session, do the Bible Study at the next session. A separate Ice-Breaker is provided for this Bible Study—which you will need to photocopy for group members.

20–30 Minutes

CARING TIME / Same Groups of 4 to 6
This is the most important part of every meeting. It is a time for sharing prayer requests and praying for one another. Be sure to stay with the agenda so that the Caring Time is not neglected.

SESSION

1

One Big Happy Family ... Right?

OBJECTIVES

To begin to get to know each other by describing our blended families.

To consider the joys and challenges of being in a blended family.

To study a passage from Romans which gives valuable insights into how to relate to those with whom you disagree (as sometimes happens in any family).

THREE-PART AGENDA

ICE-BREAKER
15 Minutes

ISSUE / BIBLE STUDY
45 Minutes

CARING TIME
30 Minutes

OPTION: If you only have 60 minutes, divide this session into two sessions, with the Bible Study section for your next time together.

ICE-BREAKER

Pass out the Handout for this session or the course book to each person. Divide the group into subgroups of 4 to 6 to get acquainted by doing the Ice-Breaker. (Photocopy pages 9 and 11 as needed.)

1. Begin by sharing your name, where you were raised, who is in your blended family, and one stress that you are feeling as a result of being in a blended family.

2. If you were to compare your blended family to a family in a TV show or movie, which one would you compare it to?
   ❒ *The Parent Trap*
   ❒ *The Brady Bunch*
   ❒ *The Addams Family*
   ❒ *The Sound of Music*
   ❒ *Stepmom*
   ❒ other:____________________________________

3. How did you hear about this group?

INTRODUCTION TO THE ISSUE

LEADER:

• Summarize these remarks (in your own words) into a brief introduction (no longer than 5 minutes).

• Be careful not to read the entire presentation to the group.

• In your presentation cover the "Discuss the Issue" questions listed on Side One of the Handout.

When a man and a woman decide to get married, they do so with great expectations. This is true for those who have never been married. It is equally true for those who remarry. However, there is a big difference between the two situations. Those who have been previously married often bring children with them into the new marriage. This invariably complicates the new marriage to one degree or another.

Such a couple has to adjust not only to each other, but also to each other's children. They do not have the luxury of an extended period alone in which to forge their new relationship. They have to balance the need to be alone with the need to be with the children (who also need time to adjust to their new family). Furthermore, relationships with extended families can take on very complex patterns. Trying to help the children adjust to a new parent and (perhaps) new siblings can be an overwhelming task.

This is not to say that blended families don't work. It is to say that they *take* work. Time and effort is needed for them to realize all their potential.

Blended families are not some exotic reality. There are many of them in the United States today and their number is growing weekly. According to the Stepfamily Association of Illinois, about one of every five U.S. families is a multi-home stepfamily. Sadly, over half of the stepfamilies in the United States divorce within 10 years.

While we have fairly clear expectations for the way relationships are supposed to work in so-called "traditional families," we are not at all sure how the relationships in blended families should function. Furthermore, certain stereotypes exist for stepparents. Stepmothers, especially, are subject to some rather cruel treatment:

- There is the wicked stepmother of Hansel and Gretel, forcing her husband to send the children into the woods to die. There is happiness only when the children come back to find that their stepmother has died (along, of course, with the evil witch, who probably is a symbol of the stepmother anyway!).

- There is Snow White's stepmother who, out of jealousy, forces Snow White to flee for her life.

- And, of course, there is Cinderella. Her stepmother was sweetness and light—until Cinderella's father died. Then her stepmother showed her true colors. She lived in luxury on her deceased husband's estate, while Cinderella was reduced to the status of a household slave.

Set against these negative stereotypes of stepparents, there is the Brady

Bunch. By virtue of endless re-runs, we are all familiar with this family. A man with three boys marries a woman with three girls, and everything works out splendidly. This husband and wife always agree on child care. All of the children are equally trusted by both parents. The memory of the boys' deceased mom (or the girls' deceased dad) never intrudes into the lives of the children. Apart from minor squabbles, the kids stick by each other. None of the boys ever say to their stepmother, "Get off my back, you're not my mother anyway." None of the girls ever try to manipulate their mother to take sides with them against their stepfather. And there's always enough money to go around ... sufficient enough to hire a witty housekeeper!

Over against all these stereotypes are real blended families which take on many forms:

- If both parents are divorced, there may be children from both marriages. Sociologists call this a "complex stepfamily." If only one spouse has children, they call it a "simple stepfamily" (although it's not!).

- The partners may have children from previous marriages, as well as some children from their own union. All of these children may live together all of the time. Or some of the children may live with another parent for some of the time.

- An ex-husband may be creating such tension that his ex-wife rarely gets to be with her child.

- The child of a financially well-off former spouse may receive opportunities that the children born from the other partner's previous marriage cannot have. This is especially tricky when all of these children share the same household.

- A man who marries a woman with three teenagers experiences a very different type of stepparenting than the one who marries a woman with an infant.

- A woman who is perceived by her husband's children as being the "other woman" (whom their mother says caused the divorce) will experience a different type of stepparenting than a woman who comes into the family well after the divorce has occurred.

Regardless of all the different forms, all stepparents have one thing in common: they will experience situations that a typical two-parent family never faces. That's why a small group for blended families is so important.

SESSION ONE HANDOUT: Blended Families

One Big Happy Family ... Right?

ICE-BREAKER / Groups of 4 to 6 / 15 Minutes

1. Begin by sharing your name, where you were raised, who is in your blended family, and one stress that you are feeling as a result of being in a blended family.

2. If you were to compare your blended family to a family in a TV show or movie, which one would you compare it to?
   ❒ *The Parent Trap*
   ❒ *The Brady Bunch*
   ❒ *The Addams Family*
   ❒ *The Sound of Music*
   ❒ *Stepmom*
   ❒ other:________________________________

3. How did you hear about this group?

DISCUSS THE ISSUE / Same Groups / 20 Minutes

After a brief introduction by the leader, take turns sharing your responses to the following questions.

1. As a child, what was your mental picture of a stepparent and why?
   ❒ Mr. and Mrs. Brady
   ❒ Cinderella's wicked stepmother
   ❒ Julie Andrews in the *Sound of Music*
   ❒ A stepparent you knew (or had)
   ❒ I never thought about stepparents.

2. What is the most unexpected discovery you have made about stepparenting?
   ❒ It is a very complex situation.
   ❒ There are fun times as well as hard times.
   ❒ It seems there are endless decisions that have to be made.
   ❒ The adjustment for the children was easier (or harder) than expected.
   ❒ The adjustment for me was easier (or harder) than expected.
   ❒ other:________________________________

3. In what ways can this group help you as you sort out the issues involved in being part of a blended family?

INTRODUCTION TO THE BIBLE STUDY

While the specific problems dealt with in this Bible passage from Romans are far removed from modern concerns, the principles involved are still very relevant. The root issue here is the way to resolve a difference of opinion over an issue that is in itself neutral (i.e., one that does not violate the moral law). Two groups within one fellowship look at the same issue in opposite ways. The question is: How can they learn to live together without violating their consciences?

Today, the kind of disagreement we usually find in blended families is probably not over food and drink. Instead, we might disagree about the proper discipline for the children or what is appropriate when relating to our former spouses. Paul's insights in this passage are most useful in developing ground rules to help us work out disagreements of this sort.

Have someone read out loud the Scripture passage. Use the reference notes that follow to enhance your understanding of the text. Then go around and let everyone take turns answering the questions.

ICE-BREAKER FOR TWO-SESSION OPTION

If you are doing the Bible Study as a separate session, start off this session by dividing this group into subgroups of 4 to 6 and answering the following questions. Photocopy and give this to the group.

We Disagree! Disagreements are the norm in relationships. This is why the New Testament spends so much time discussing ways to resolve conflict between people. Certainly in any healthy family there will be disagreements. How we disagree (and how we resolve our differences) is the key thing. Answer the following questions and share your responses with the group.

1. Thinking back on disagreements you have had as a couple, try to recall the following:
   - ❒ the first thing you disagreed about
   - ❒ the most trivial thing you have disagreed about
   - ❒ the funniest thing you have disagreed about

2. What works best for you in resolving differences of opinion?
   - ❒ taking time out
   - ❒ both giving way
   - ❒ listening carefully to each other
   - ❒ agreeing to disagree
   - ❒ still trying to find the best way
   - ❒ laughter
   - ❒ shouting the loudest
   - ❒ avoiding sensitive issues
   - ❒ tears
   - ❒ other:________________
   - ❒ the willingness to admit being wrong
   - ❒ alternating who gets to win the disagreement

SESSION ONE BIBLE STUDY

***14** Accept him whose faith is weak, without passing judgment on disputable matters. [2]One man's faith allows him to eat everything, but another man, whose faith is weak, eats only vegetables. [3]The man who eats everything must not look down on him who does not, and the man who does not eat everything must not condemn the man who does, for God has accepted him. [4]Who are you to judge someone else's servant? To his own master he stands or falls. And he will stand, for the Lord is able to make him stand. ...*

[13]Therefore let us stop passing judgment on one another. Instead, make up your mind not to put any stumbling block or obstacle in your brother's way. [14]As one who is in the Lord Jesus, I am fully convinced that no food is unclean in itself. But if anyone regards something as unclean, then for him it is unclean. [15]If your brother is distressed because of what you eat, you are no longer acting in love. Do not by your eating destroy your brother for whom Christ died. [16]Do not allow what you consider good to be spoken of as evil. [17]For the kingdom of God is not a matter of eating and drinking, but of righteousness, peace and joy in the Holy Spirit, [18]because anyone who serves Christ in this way is pleasing to God and approved by men.

[19]Let us therefore make every effort to do what leads to peace and to mutual edification. [20]Do not destroy the work of God for the sake of food. All food is clean, but it is wrong for a man to eat anything that causes someone else to stumble. [21]It is better not to eat meat or drink wine or to do anything else that will cause your brother to fall.

[22]So whatever you believe about these things keep between yourself and God. Blessed is the man who does not condemn himself by what he approves. [23]But the man who has doubts is condemned if he eats, because his eating is not from faith; and everything that does not come from faith is sin.

Romans 14:1–4,13–23

1. Looking through this passage as a whole, what phrases highlight the type of attitudes that Christians are to have (or are not to have) toward those with whom they disagree?

2. Take each of the attitudes identified in question 1 and discuss how they could apply to disagreement within a blended family. Which attitude especially challenges you?

3. Of all the attitudes and actions suggested here by Paul, which ones do you feel you need to work on?
   - ❒ to stop judging another's behavior or values
   - ❒ to keep quiet about my point of view on certain issues
   - ❒ to make the decision not to upset another person
   - ❒ to make the effort required for peace and harmony
   - ❒ to make room for another opinion to coexist with mine
   - ❒ to stop what I'm doing for the sake of others

REFERENCE NOTES

Romans 14:1–4,13–23

14:1 *faith is weak.* These are the people who do not feel assured that their faith allows them to do certain things. The issue is not a lack of faith in Christ. Both the weak and the strong are authentically Christian.

14:3 *for God has accepted him.* The abstainer cannot condemn those who indulge, since no one can presume to judge a person God has accepted.

14:4 It is Christ himself who is concerned whether the strong Christian continues in faith or falls away.

14:13 *stumbling block.* A new theme is introduced into the discussion: the liberty of the strong can, in fact, be detrimental to others. What appears to them as an innocent pleasure or action may cause pain, shock, outrage, or even hurt to the more scrupulous.

14:14 *regards something as unclean.* For those believers who have not yet been convinced that Christ abolished the ceremonial law of the Old Testament (even though the food is not *objectively* unclean), it is *subjectively* so for that person.

14:15 *destroy.* But by exercising this liberty, it is possible that "the weak in faith will be grievously hurt, he will have the integrity of his faith ... and obedience destroyed, and his salvation put at risk" (Cranfield).

14:17 *righteousness, peace and joy.* The kingdom of God does not consist of selfish actions (such as eating and drinking what one wants, regardless of the scruples of one's brothers and sisters). Instead, the kingdom of God consists of righteousness—giving God and others their due (especially in this case, understanding and consideration); peace—that which makes for the highest good for another (especially here, right relationships); and joy—that which comes by seeking the good of others. Paul urges outward actions motivated by the needs of others, rather than a self-oriented insistence on personal "rights."

14:23 *faith.* Here "faith" signifies a sort of inner freedom or liberty that comes from knowing that what one is doing is in accord with Christian faith in general.

sin. When a Christian does something that is inherently neither bad or good *without* a sense of inner liberty, it becomes sin to that Christian. Strong Christians need to know this when they urge the weak to partake against their conscience.

CARING TIME

Take time now to share any personal prayer requests. Start out by asking everyone to answer this question:

"How can we help you in prayer this week?"

Take turns praying for each other, remembering the requests that have been shared. If you would like to pray in silence, say the word "Amen" when you have finished your prayer, so that the next person will know when to start. At the close, join hands and pray this prayer together.

"Dear God, Thank you for the gift of my spouse and my family.
Give us your wisdom in dealing with the many
decisions and conflicts that arise in daily life.
Help us to always make you the center of
our family so that we may bring glory to you.
Thank you also for bringing this group together.
Help us to become a supportive, loving
and caring group that can build up each
family represented here.
Amen."

LEADER:

If applicable, have the group use the extra space on this page for group prayer requests.

SESSION

2

Blended Families vs. First Families

OBJECTIVES

To become aware of some of the key differences between our first family and being part of a blended family.

To get in touch with some of the feelings we have in this situation.

To examine a passage from Romans that identifies the perspective we need to cope successfully with the realities of blended families.

THREE-PART AGENDA

ICE-BREAKER
15 Minutes

ISSUE / BIBLE STUDY
45 Minutes

CARING TIME
30 Minutes

OPTION: If you only have 60 minutes, divide this session into two sessions, with the Bible Study section for your next time together.

ICE-BREAKER

Pass out the Handout for this session or the course book to each person. Divide the group into subgroups of 4 to 6 to get acquainted by doing the Ice-Breaker. (Photocopy pages 17 and 19 as needed.)

1. If you could become a child again and pick a TV family to grow up in, which family would you pick? What do you especially like about the family you picked?
   - ❒ The Cleavers *(Leave It To Beaver)*
   - ❒ The Taylors *(Home Improvement)*
   - ❒ The Seavers *(Growing Pains)*
   - ❒ The Huxtables *(The Cosby Show)*
   - ❒ The Barones *(Everybody Loves Raymond)*
   - ❒ The Clampetts *(Beverly Hillbillies)*
   - ❒ The Camdens *(7th Heaven)*
   - ❒ other:____________________

2. What is one way you hope your present family could be like the TV family you chose?

INTRODUCTION TO THE ISSUE

LEADER:

• Summarize these remarks (in your own words) into a brief introduction (no longer than 5 minutes).

• Be careful not to read the entire presentation to the group.

• In your presentation cover the "Discuss the Issue" questions listed on Side One of the Handout.

Part of the problem with the Brady Bunch was the unreality concerning their situation. If the TV show is to be believed (and it is not), there was no discernible difference between the eight Bradys and any other family of eight. But the fact is, the Brady family was different. It combined two quite different family histories, replete with the pain that came from the death of two spouses (not to mention the disorientation that comes from starting a new lifestyle). Also, each half of the new Brady family brought along an army of relatives and friends unknown to the other half. The blending of these two different families had to have been complex and demanding.

A person in love, marrying into a blended family, may simply feel that he or she is marrying a wonderful person who happens to have a couple of kids. It soon becomes obvious, however, that the kids are no mere appendages to the relationship! They become a central part of its definition ... as does an ex-wife or ex-husband ... as do strained financial and logistical arrangements. In short, the extended honeymoon (that childless couples often experience) is quickly curtailed by the constant, everyday needs and demands of blended family life. Things just don't operate as smoothly as the Brady Bunch model. Real blended families must deal with the fact:

- That at least one adult in the house is considered an outsider by the children.
- That, initially at least, the parent-child bond may be stronger than the bond between the spouses.
- That generally there are financial commitments to former spouses, and perhaps children who live outside the home.
- That some people in the blended family may feel out of place in the very place that is supposed to be their home.
- That holidays, rather than being a time of joy, become logistical nightmares, as various children are shuttled off to various parents at various times.

Consider the following true situation:

> Bob had never been married when he met June, a recently divorced woman with three teenage children who lived with her. Bob and June grew to love each other and decided to marry. Bob knew things could be difficult (because June's ex-husband was very erratic regarding child-support payments, and frequently treated June and the kids in an emotionally abusive way). The ex-husband would threaten to take custody, claiming June was an unfit mother. He would arrange for the kids to visit with him, only to cancel out at the last moment. While

Bob knew the kids were deeply angry at their dad, he also knew they loved him and resented it when their mother spoke badly of him. He also knew that June's self-image was fragile from the emotional battering she had endured in her former marriage.

Soon after their wedding, June suffered a mild stroke, leaving Bob responsible for the daily needs of the kids. He felt overwhelmed by the physical energy and time required to care for three kids, work at his job, and visit his wife in the hospital. It was all the harder since the kids were unresponsive to him and expressed no visible appreciation for his efforts to keep things together.

June recovered and resumed the role she had in the household prior to the stroke. This was a relief to Bob, but he still wondered what he could do to build some bridges of love with June's kids. The oldest boy was polite but distant. The girl could be sarcastic. The youngest boy seemed to ignore Bob when he was around, and kept talking about wanting to live with his dad. At least twice that first year, his dad said he could come and live with him, but backed out of the arrangement at the last minute.

A few months after June's hospital stay, her daughter became pregnant. Her father (who was supposed to provide medical care for the children) refused to pay any of the expenses, accusing June of bringing on the whole mess because she was always a lousy mother anyway. June was devastated by his constant verbal assaults, the financial pressures that were mounting rapidly, and her worry over her daughter. Bob felt helpless. He was angry at June's daughter for bringing on this latest round of conflict, but really knew she was hurting deeply too. He was furious at June's ex-husband, and distressed over the way June was reacting to all that was happening. Meanwhile, June's youngest boy was having serious trouble at school, which no one was aware of until June was notified by the school principal that her son was close to being expelled.

Soon after this, Bob and June celebrated their first wedding anniversary.

As this case study demonstrates, there are many different challenges and issues that can come up in the life of a blended family. Accepting the reality of these problems is the first step in learning to build a successful family life. Once the problems are recognized, then solutions can be found with the help of all family members. Thus, difficulties can result in bringing a blended family closer together, rather than farther apart.

Blended Families vs. First Families

ICE-BREAKER / Groups of 4 to 6 / 15 Minutes

1. If you could become a child again and pick a TV family to grow up in, which family would you pick? What do you especially like about the family you picked?
   ❒ The Cleavers *(Leave It To Beaver)*
   ❒ The Taylors *(Home Improvement)*
   ❒ The Seavers *(Growing Pains)*
   ❒ The Huxtables *(The Cosby Show)*
   ❒ The Barones *(Everybody Loves Raymond)*
   ❒ The Clampetts *(Beverly Hillbillies)*
   ❒ The Camdens *(7th Heaven)*
   ❒ other:______________________________

2. What is one way you hope your present family could be like the TV family you chose?

DISCUSS THE ISSUE / Same Groups / 20 Minutes

After a brief introduction by the leader, take turns sharing your responses to the following questions.

1. With what in Bob and June's experience can you identify? In what other ways have you found blended family life to be different from first family life?

2. Right now, how do you feel about this "gap" between the "Brady Bunch" family and the realities you live with?
   ❒ What "gap"? I *am* living happily ever after.
   ❒ I am frustrated that things are so different than what I expected.
   ❒ The fun times are especially cherished, since they are so hard-won.
   ❒ I wish the kids would get their acts together.
   ❒ When I was younger, I could have handled this.
   ❒ other:______________________________

3. When feelings of frustration surface, how do you usually react?
   ❒ I explore.
   ❒ I exercise.
   ❒ I blame.
   ❒ I take a pill.
   ❒ I withdraw.
   ❒ I get mean.
   ❒ I run away.
   ❒ I go to bed.
   ❒ I get silent.
   ❒ I cry.
   ❒ I pray.
   ❒ other:______________
   ❒ I throw up my hands and say "What the heck."

INTRODUCTION TO THE BIBLE STUDY

In this passage from Romans, Paul begins by focusing on how we are to respond to God. Our response to God is based on what God has done for us in Jesus Christ (which was the subject of the first half of Romans). Paul begins the second half of Romans (with this passage) by focusing on our place within the Christian community: How we are to view ourselves and use our gifts in that context. His teaching provides valuable insights into both who we are, and how we are to relate successfully to others in the family of God. These insights will also stand us in good stead with our blended families.

Have someone read the Scripture passage out loud. Remember to use the reference notes to enhance your understanding of the text. Then go around on the questions, and let everyone share their answers.

ICE-BREAKER FOR TWO-SESSION OPTION

If you are doing the Bible Study as a separate session, start off this session by dividing this group into subgroups of 4 to 6 and answering the following questions. Photocopy and give this to the group.

TV Families Never Fight. Go back to the TV family that you picked in the opening Ice-Breaker of this session. Answer the following questions as if you were a member of that family:

1. Over what issues does your TV family disagree?

❐ money ❐ discipline ❐ bad habits
❐ nothing ❐ career ❐ everything
❐ sex ❐ in-laws ❐ other:____________

2. How does your TV family settle its disagreements?

❐ They seem to know the right thing and eventually do it.
❐ They all have unlimited good will, which rescues them.
❐ They just laugh it off.
❐ The issues are always trivial, so it's no big deal.
❐ Nobody is ever seriously out of line.
❐ other:____________

3. What is one thing you want to say to your TV family?

❐ You've got to be kidding.
❐ I wish it were so.
❐ Where can I learn to be so witty and clever?
❐ Thanks for the memories.
❐ other:____________

SESSION TWO BIBLE STUDY

***12** Therefore, I urge you, brothers, in view of God's mercy, to offer your*
bodies as living sacrifices, holy and pleasing to God—this is your spir-
itual act of worship. 2Do not conform any longer to the pattern of this world, but be trans-
formed by the renewing of your mind. Then you will be able to test and approve what
God's will is—his good, pleasing and perfect will.
3For by the grace given me I say to every one of you: Do not think of yourself more
highly than you ought, but rather think of yourself with sober judgment, in accordance
with the measure of faith God has given you. 4Just as each of us has one body with many
members, and these members do not all have the same function, 5so in Christ we who are
many form one body, and each member belongs to all the others. 6We have different gifts,
according to the grace given us. If a man's gift is prophesying, let him use it in proportion
to his faith. 7If it is serving, let him serve; if it is teaching, let him teach; 8if it is encourag-
ing, let him encourage; if it is contributing to the needs of others, let him give generous-
ly; if it is leadership, let him govern diligently; if it is showing mercy, let him do it cheer-
fully.

Romans 12:1–8

1. According to verses 1–2, what are the three ways we are to respond to God? What does each command mean?

2. What happens to us (both adults and kids) when we conform to the mindset of the world around us (as promoted by television, for example)? How would we think about ourselves? What tensions would this introduce into a family?

3. According to verses 3–8, how are we supposed to think about ourselves?
- ❒ Don't be arrogant, but don't minimize my gifts.
- ❒ I need others, and others need me.
- ❒ I must do my part in my family with enthusiasm.
- ❒ The person who doesn't do his or her part hurts the whole family.
- ❒ other: ____________________

4. Which of the following comments describes where God fits into your present situation?
- ❒ He doesn't fit in at all.
- ❒ That's one reason I'm coming to this group—to try to find out!
- ❒ God is present when things get the darkest.
- ❒ My trust in him gives me a sense of perspective.
- ❒ I need to get back in touch with God.
- ❒ other: ____________________

REFERENCE NOTES

Romans 12:1–8

12:1 ***in view of God's mercy.*** A Christian's motivation to obedience is overwhelming gratitude for God's mercy.

12:2 ***be transformed.*** The force of the verb is "continue to let yourself be transformed"; i.e., a continuous action by the Holy Spirit which goes on for a lifetime. A Christian's responsibility is to stay open to this sanctification process.

renewing of your mind. Develop a spiritual sensitivity and perception—learn to look at life on the basis of God's view of reality. Paul emphasizes the need to develop *understanding* of God's ways.

test and approve. Christians are called to a responsible freedom of choice and action, based on the inner renewing work of the Holy Spirit.

12:3 ***sober judgment.*** The command is to know oneself (especially one's gifts) accurately, rather than to have too high an opinion of oneself in comparison to others. This attitude enables a body of believers to use their gifts together in harmonious ministry.

measure of faith. Believers are not to measure themselves against others, but against the standard God has given them in their faith. Thus they can achieve a true estimate of themselves.

12:4–5 By means of a word picture that could be understood in all cultures—the body—Paul defines the nature of the Christian community: Diverse gifts, but all part of one body, the body of Christ.

12:6 ***gifts.*** Those endowments given by God to every believer by grace (grace and gifts come from the same root word) to be used in God's service. The gifts listed here (or in 1 Corinthians 12 or Ephesians 4:11–12) are not meant to be exhaustive or absolute, since no gift list overlaps completely.

12:7 ***serving.*** The special capacity for rendering practical service to the needy.

12:8 ***mercy.*** "The person whose special function is, on behalf of the congregation, to tend the sick, relieve the pain, or care for the aged or disabled" (Cranfield). Note that four of the seven gifts involve practical assistance to the needy.

CARING TIME

Remember that this time is for developing and expressing your caring for each other. You can do this by sharing any personal prayer requests and praying for each other's needs. Start by answering the question:

"In what area of your life would you like to be transformed by the renewing of your mind?"

Then share any other prayer requests and take turns praying for each other. Close by taking a few minutes for each group member to say a brief prayer of thanks for his or her blended family and for the gifts that God has given to each family member.

LEADER:

If applicable, have the group use the extra space on this page for group prayer requests.

SESSION

3

The Children

OBJECTIVES

To explore some of the issues involved in successful stepparenting.

To examine a passage from Romans that gives us insight into the nature of good relationships.

THREE-PART AGENDA

ICE-BREAKER
15 Minutes

ISSUE / BIBLE STUDY
45 Minutes

CARING TIME
30 Minutes

OPTION: If you only have 60 minutes, divide this session into two sessions, with the Bible Study section for your next time together.

ICE-BREAKER

Pass out the Handout for this session or the course book to each person. Divide the group into subgroups of 4 to 6 to do the Ice-Breaker. (Photocopy pages 25 and 27 as needed.)

1. Create a "Coat of Arms" that reflects your family heritage. Cut a piece of construction paper into the form of a shield. With a colored pen, divide it into four sections.

   - In the first section, write two strengths you gained from your father (e.g., the ability to work hard, and a commitment to family).
   - In the second section, write two strengths you gained from your mother (e.g., sensitivity to others, and willingness to serve others).
   - In the third section, write two words that describe your place in the family when you were a child (e.g., the achiever and reconciler).
   - In the fourth section, write two words that describe your childhood (e.g., endless activity and lots of books).

   Share what you wrote or drew with the other members of the subgroup.

2. What did this exercise show you about the importance of your parents in your life? About your childhood? What does this say to you about your own children and stepchildren?

INTRODUCTION TO THE ISSUE

LEADER:

• Summarize these remarks (in your own words) into a brief introduction (no longer than 5 minutes).

• Be careful not to read the entire presentation to the group.

• In your presentation cover the "Discuss the Issue" questions listed on Side One of the Handout.

We sometimes think that stepparenting is a new issue, brought about by the increased rates of divorce and remarriage occurring in today's world. It keeps things in perspective to realize that in nineteenth century America, 25% of all children were raised in stepfamilies, mainly as the result of the death of a parent. The problems of stepparenting are not all that new, it seems.

The following suggestions for stepparents are adapted from a booklet entitled, *Yours, Mine, and Ours: Tips for Stepparents* by Sharyn Duffin (a U.S. Department of Health, Education and Welfare publication).

Before marriage:

- Discuss the changes in lifestyle that bringing two families together will involve.
- Get to know each other's children somewhat.
- Watch how your prospective mate relates to your children. What principles have each of you used to rear your own children? How do they differ?
- Prepare your children for the practical effects of remarriage. Discuss such things as: the new living arrangements, their time with the non-custodial parent, the new siblings they will have, etc. Give them ample opportunity to express their fears. Seek to calm these where possible. Young children, for example, may fear that since you love this new person, you will not love them anymore. Or they fear that they will not be allowed to stay with you anymore. Older teens wonder whether they will have a room they like, or if there will be enough money for college finances.
- Discuss family finances with your future spouse. What financial obligations do you already have? What ones will you have in the future?
- Sometimes a prospective mate has hopes that you will not only be a better spouse than his or her former one, but a better parent for the children as well. This is an unfair and unrealistic expectation—one that (from the child's perspective) you are almost guaranteed to be unable to meet. Don't accept that type of pressure.

After marriage:

- Accept the fact that children need time to adjust to a stepparent and stepsiblings. You need time to adjust too. Don't expect too much too soon. If your spouse's child gets angry at you (saying you have no right to tell them anything because you're not his or her real parent), acknowledge that this is so. Go on to point out that things are hard for all of you right now, but that you all must find a way to live together.

- Don't try to replace a lost parent. You can't do it, no matter how cruel or abusive you feel the natural parent was (or is). However, over time, you can become an adult friend and mentor.

- Accept that you will be compared to the absent parent, and that you will come up short. Be prepared to be tested, manipulated and challenged. Don't expect "thank you's" for your services. Don't expect Mother's Day or Father's Day gifts. The children may simply be emotionally unable to see you as a mother or father figure. Yours will be a thankless job for the most part.

- Don't feel guilty if you don't love your stepchildren as you do your own, or if they don't love you as a parent. Sometimes even natural parents don't like their kids! Instead, strive for respect, consideration and integrity in your relationship with them. Love may grow as a by-product.

- Be in agreement with your mate about household rules and discipline.

- Realize that young teenagers are generally the most difficult to stepparent. Studies indicate that stepparenting is hardest for couples who marry when there are children between 9–15 years old. While your need as a new spouse is to establish new family ties, they are struggling with their need to form a separate identity from the family. Both sets of goals are important, even though they are at odds with one another. Don't force an artificial togetherness.

- Each person in the new family needs something that is really their own, such as a room. This will give each of you a sense of physical belonging in this household.

- Communicate! Acknowledge and deal with problems immediately.

- Get outside help as needed. No one can be expected to become an instant parent without experiencing stress and confusion. Visit a personal or family counselor (or a support group) when things start to become difficult.

- Be flexible. The only sure thing about stepparenting is that what works now will have to change next year!

These suggestions themselves demonstrate the complexity of stepparenting. This challenge will never be an easy task, but with patience, time and understanding you can develop a good relationship with your stepchildren.

SESSION THREE HANDOUT: Blended Families

The Children

ICE-BREAKER / Groups of 4 to 6 / 15 Minutes

1. Create a "Coat of Arms" that reflects your family heritage. Cut a piece of construction paper into the form of a shield. With a colored pen, divide it into four sections.

   - In the first section, write two strengths you gained from your father (e.g., the ability to work hard, and a commitment to family).

   - In the second section, write two strengths you gained from your mother (e.g., sensitivity to others, and willingness to serve others).

   - In the third section, write two words that describe your place in the family when you were a child (e.g., the achiever and reconciler).

   - In the fourth section, write two words that describe your childhood (e.g., endless activity and lots of books).

   Share what you wrote or drew with the other members of the subgroup.

2. What did this exercise show you about the importance of your parents in your life? About your childhood? What does this say to you about your own children and stepchildren?

DISCUSS THE ISSUE / Same Groups / 20 Minutes

After a brief introduction by the leader, take turns sharing your responses to the following questions.

1. Which of these suggestions makes good sense to you and why?

2. What have been some of the sources of tension in your relationship with your stepchildren? How have you dealt with these?

3. What would you add to this list of suggestions about having a good relationship with stepchildren?

INTRODUCTION TO THE BIBLE STUDY

It is important to understand that Paul's intention in this passage from Romans 12 is not to overwhelm his readers with a lot of new rules (which they are supposed to follow in order to be right with God). That is not what Christianity is all about. Rather, his aim is to describe the character of a person who is being "transformed by the renewal" of his or her mind (Romans 12:2) through the grace of God. The principles Paul describes here are of great value in becoming better stepparents.

Listen for these principles to live by as someone reads the Scripture passage out loud. Then go around on each question and let everyone share their answer.

ICE-BREAKER FOR TWO-SESSION OPTION

If you are doing the Bible Study as a separate session, start off this session by dividing this group into subgroups of 4 to 6 and answering the following questions. Photocopy and give this to the group.

Relatives, Relatives. Relatives are the bane and blessing of children. Recall your childhood experience by answering the following questions and sharing your memories with the rest of the group.

1. When you were a child, who was a favorite relative? What made that person your favorite?

2. What large family events did you enjoy most as a child: Christmas? Family reunions? Sundays when your uncle's family visited? What made it so much fun?

3. Recall one thing that you didn't like as a child at big family gatherings. (For example: not being allowed to interrupt grown-up conversation, or getting messy kisses from one particular aunt.)

SESSION THREE BIBLE STUDY

9 Love must be sincere. Hate what is evil; cling to what is good. 10 Be devoted to one another in brotherly love. Honor one another above yourselves. 11 Never be lacking in zeal, but keep your spiritual fervor, serving the Lord. 12 Be joyful in hope, patient in affliction, faithful in prayer. 13 Share with God's people who are in need. Practice hospitality.

14 Bless those who persecute you; bless and do not curse. 15 Rejoice with those who rejoice; mourn with those who mourn. 16 Live in harmony with one another. Do not be proud, but be willing to associate with people of low position. Do not be conceited.

17 Do not repay anyone evil for evil. Be careful to do what is right in the eyes of everybody. 18 If it is possible, as far as it depends on you, live at peace with everyone. 19 Do not take revenge, my friends, but leave room for God's wrath, for it is written: "It is mine to avenge; I will repay," says the Lord. 20 On the contrary:

> ***"If your enemy is hungry, feed him;***
> ***if he is thirsty, give him something to drink.***
> ***In doing this, you will heap burning coals on his head."***

21 Do not be overcome by evil, but overcome evil with good.

Romans 12:9–21

1. There are over 25 principles for behavior found in this passage! Try to identify all the things that Paul tells us to *do* and *not to do.* A scribe will keep track of the group's insights.

2. Given these guidelines about the way we should live, which two are the *easiest* for you, in terms of relating to your stepchildren? Which two are the *hardest*? Why?

3. What is the place of discipline, punishment and negative feelings in this pattern?

4. We can't give what we don't have. Where do you find a source of love and peace in your life that enables you to live like this with your stepchildren?

5. You might be feeling, "It's easy for Paul to write this way. He never had any stepchildren!" In what way can this group support you as you try to apply these principles to your particular situation?

REFERENCE NOTES

Romans 12:9–21

12:9 *Love.* *Agape,* self-giving action on behalf of others made possible by God's Spirit.

sincere. Genuine, not counterfeit or showy. It is possible to pretend (even to one's self) to love others.

12:10 *brotherly love.* A second word for love is used here, *philadelphia,* denoting the tender affection found in families, now said to be appropriate to those in the church—which is the Christian's new family.

Honor. Since other Christians are in union with Christ, they are to be honored.

12:11 *fervor.* This Greek word is also used of water which is boiling (or of metal, like copper, which is glowing red hot).

12:12 What makes it possible to endure affliction is a joyful hope in one's secure inheritance in the age to come, coupled with daily, continuous prayer.

12:13 To be "renewed" is not just an interior matter of mind and emotions, but involves concrete outer action such as giving to those in need.

12:14 A clear example of how "renewal of our minds" is opposed to "the pattern of this world."

12:15 Believers are also to share those most deeply human moments with their persecutors.

12:16 Christians ought to provide a model of harmony for the world around them. Avoiding haughtiness, they are to associate with all types of people, regardless of social status or wealth.

12:20 *burning coals.* Providing kindness of every sort to one's enemies may induce the kind of inner shame that leads to repentance, and hence to reconciliation and true friendship.

12:21 People who retaliate have allowed evil to overcome them. They have given in to their evil desires and have become like their enemy.

CARING TIME

Begin by sharing any personal prayer requests and then answering the question:

"How do you need God's help and strength in facing the challenge of parenting your stepchildren?"

Go around and let each person pray for the person on their right, remembering the concerns that have been shared. If someone prefers to pray silently, have them say "Amen" out loud to indicate their preference. Start with this sentence:

"Dear God, I want to talk with you about my friend ___________________."

Close by thanking God for bringing you together as a group and asking him to help you grow through the conflict and difficulties of being a step-parent.

LEADER:

If applicable, have the group use the extra space on this page for group prayer requests.

SESSION

The "Ex" Factor

OBJECTIVES

To reflect on some of the common pitfalls when it comes to relating to the ex-spouse.

To discuss ways that can help smooth out that relationship.

To examine a passage from Colossians that explores the connection between spirituality and relationships.

THREE-PART AGENDA

ICE-BREAKER
15 Minutes

ISSUE / BIBLE STUDY
45 Minutes

CARING TIME
30 Minutes

OPTION: If you only have 60 minutes, divide this session into two sessions, with the Bible Study section for your next time together.

ICE-BREAKER

Pass out the Handout for this session or the course book to each person. Divide the group into subgroups of 4 to 6 to do the Ice-Breaker. (Photocopy pages 33 and 35 as needed.)

1. When you were a kid, how did you feel about fairy tales that ended with, "They got married and lived happily ever after"?
   - ❒ Marriage must be heaven.
   - ❒ Whoever said that doesn't know my family.
   - ❒ I can't wait to be married, because then I'll be happy.
   - ❒ Fairy tales lie.
   - ❒ Of course, that's the way it is.
   - ❒ Yuck, I hate romantic stories.
   - ❒ After marriage, I guess nothing else happens.

2. When you were a teenager, what play, movie, popular song, or famous person made a big impression on you, regarding what love and marriage was supposed to be like?

3. What ideal about love and marriage did the movie (etc.) fix in your mind? Since then, what has your experience taught you about what is true (and what is false) about that ideal?

INTRODUCTION TO THE ISSUE

LEADER:

• Summarize these remarks (in your own words) into a brief introduction (no longer than 5 minutes).

• Be careful not to read the entire presentation to the group.

• In your presentation cover the "Discuss the Issue" questions listed on Side One of the Handout.

While the "wicked stepmother" image is firmly embedded in our culture, the "wicked ex" is a fact of life for many stepparents! This is not always true, of course, but the fact that you and/or your spouse were formerly married *is* a factor in all remarriages. Patterns of relating (developed over the years that the partners were together) are not automatically canceled out when a new marriage begins. Expectations about husbands and wives (cultivated in that first marriage) may be unconsciously carried along into a second marriage. How the former partner is getting along in his or her life can have a dramatic effect on the peace and harmony of the new marriage.

The overall influence of the former marriage upon a new marriage is especially strong when there are children from that former marriage. Divorce may have ended the marriage, but some type of relationship has to continue between the former partners (because of the continuing needs of their children). Issues that are difficult to deal with, even when two people are married—child discipline, school plans, college expenses, wedding plans and medical crises—become all the more fraught with tension when the parents are divorced and remarried.

- Ex-spouses lack the time, the intimacy (and, often, the trust) to interact effectively when it comes to difficult issues.

- It is not uncommon for one spouse to assume the worst about the other.

- Unresolved issues from the past make it difficult to come to mutually supportive arrangements in the present.

- Sometimes an ex has great difficulty in getting over resentment of the new spouse (whom he or she feels is responsible for ruining the former marriage).

Child care often becomes the battleground on which these issues are fought. As a result, the whole blended family experiences stress.

Since "ex" situations come in so many forms, it is impossible to generate guidelines that will universally help all remarried couples to avoid difficulties. However, there are some insights that are applicable to most situations.

- Both you and your spouse need to plan financial arrangements with your ex-spouses *before* the bills come due! For example, if nothing is stated about college costs in the divorce decree, start negotiations concerning these expenses while the kids are still in the first years of high school. This will give you enough time to think, discuss, argue, and plan in relative calm. Trying to do so the month before Johnny is supposed to start Yale can lead to trouble!

- Some tensions arise simply because you (or your spouse) fail to communicate adequately with your ex about arrangements for the kids (whether it be for visitation, expenses, holiday plans, transportation or whatever). You assume one thing, but your ex assumes something else, and so the trouble begins. Advance planning on your part will alleviate these kinds of unnecessary difficulties.

- Do not indulge in "ex-smashing" in any form with stepchildren, or with people who are mutual acquaintances.

- Allow your spouse to be responsible for contacting his or her ex about matters of child care, finances, etc. that need to be worked out. Trying to step into that role will only lead to resentment from both parties.

- When you need to interact with an ex, be clear, honest, and keep to the point under discussion. Treat him or her with dignity, regardless of how you feel at the moment. Insults and heated exchanges will only come back to haunt you.

- Realize that there will be things you don't like which you are powerless to change. You cannot change your ex's attitudes or actions. You cannot change the emotional response your spouse has toward his or her ex. You probably cannot have the terms of the divorce altered. You *do* have the power to work on your own attitudes and actions in such situations. You can learn that the emotional barometer of your life is not controlled by the highs and lows of the ex (either yours or your spouse's).

Marriage has been defined as a school for sanctification—a place where the rough edges of our lives are exposed and smoothed out. If that is true, then blended family marriage is post-graduate work! The additional dynamics of an ex-spouse relationship guarantee that you will discover you are capable of feeling, saying and doing things you never believed possible beforehand! You will need to continually seek spiritual and emotional support as you face the challenge of following the guidelines discussed in this session.

SESSION FOUR HANDOUT: Blended Families

The "Ex" Factor

ICE-BREAKER / Groups of 4 to 6 / 15 Minutes

1. When you were a kid, how did you feel about fairy tales that ended with, "They got married and lived happily ever after"?
   ❒ Marriage must be heaven.
   ❒ Whoever said that doesn't know my family.
   ❒ I can't wait to be married, because then I'll be happy.
   ❒ Fairy tales lie.
   ❒ Of course, that's the way it is.
   ❒ Yuck, I hate romantic stories.
   ❒ After marriage, I guess nothing else happens.

2. When you were a teenager, what play, movie, popular song, or famous person made a big impression on you, regarding what love and marriage was supposed to be like?

3. What ideal about love and marriage did the movie (etc.) fix in your mind? Since then, what has your experience taught you about what is true (and what is false) about that ideal?

DISCUSS THE ISSUE / Same Groups / 20 Minutes

After a brief introduction by the leader, take turns sharing your responses to the following questions.

1. Which of the guidelines presented are especially important and why? From your experience, are there other guidelines you would offer?

2. On a scale of 1 (none at all) to 10 (almost daily), how much interaction do you still have with your former spouse? Your mate's former spouse?

3. Again, on a scale of 1 (at peace) to 10 (at war), how do you get along with both ex-spouses?

4. What are some of the issues that you face with an "ex" at this moment? What has helped? What doesn't help?

INTRODUCTION TO THE BIBLE STUDY

In his letter to the Colossians, Paul confronts false teachers who felt that the faith of the Colossians was inferior to their own particular brand of spirituality. These false teachers were not concerned about relationships. The form of spirituality they advocated was rooted in the prideful assumption that one could control spiritual forces through religious practices and rituals. This is far removed from true spirituality, which glories in Christ and reflects him in everyday relationships. It is in difficult relationships (such as with ex-spouses) that we truly learn what it means to be gracious, loving and forgiving.

Listen while someone reads out loud the Scripture passage taken from the third chapter of Colossians. Then go around and take turns answering each of the questions that follow.

ICE-BREAKER FOR TWO-SESSION OPTION

If you are doing the Bible Study as a separate session, start off this session by dividing this group into subgroups of 4 to 6 and answering the following questions. Photocopy and give this to the group.

What a "Pain." Think back to your childhood and recall a person you didn't particularly like (this could be a teacher, a relative, another kid, even a sibling). Answer the following questions with that person in mind:

1. Who was this person who was such a "pain" to you? Why didn't you like this person? Was he or she:

- ❒ arrogant
- ❒ a loud mouth
- ❒ obnoxious
- ❒ "too good to be true"
- ❒ just someone I didn't like
- ❒ a bully
- ❒ a tattletale
- ❒ mean
- ❒ other:________________

2. How did you treat him or her?

- ❒ avoided them
- ❒ bullied them
- ❒ made life miserable
- ❒ shunned them
- ❒ bad-mouthed them
- ❒ argued with them
- ❒ let them control me
- ❒ other:________________

3. Were you ever considered a "pain" by anyone and why?

4. What's your strategy with an obnoxious salesperson?

- ❒ pretend he or she isn't there
- ❒ agree with everything, but buy nothing
- ❒ talk even faster than him or her
- ❒ raise endless arguments
- ❒ walk away
- ❒ play deaf (or dumb)
- ❒ buy what he or she is selling

SESSION FOUR BIBLE STUDY

***3** Since, then, you have been raised with Christ, set your hearts on things*
above, where Christ is seated at the right hand of God. 2Set your minds on
things above, not on earthly things. 3For you died, and your life is now hidden with Christ
in God. 4When Christ, who is your life, appears, then you also will appear with him in glory.
5Put to death, therefore, whatever belongs to your earthly nature: sexual immorality,
impurity, lust, evil desires and greed, which is idolatry. 6Because of these, the wrath of
God is coming. 7You used to walk in these ways, in the life you once lived. 8But now you
must rid yourselves of all such things as these: anger, rage, malice, slander, and filthy lan-
guage from your lips. 9Do not lie to each other, since you have taken off your old self with
its practices 10and have put on the new self, which is being renewed in knowledge in the
image of its Creator. 11Here there is no Greek or Jew, circumcised or uncircumcised, bar-
barian, Scythian, slave or free, but Christ is all, and is in all.
12Therefore, as God's chosen people, holy and dearly loved, clothe yourselves with
compassion, kindness, humility, gentleness and patience. 13Bear with each other and for-
give whatever grievances you may have against one another. Forgive as the Lord forgave
you. 14And over all these virtues put on love, which binds them all together in perfect unity.

Colossians 3:1–14

1. What is the source of true spirituality (vv. 1–4)? How can these truths help us to relate lovingly to other people (even those we are in conflict with)?

2. Make a list contrasting the qualities we are to *avoid* with those we are to *embrace.* How do these qualities impact our relationships?

3. In what way(s) are these positive qualities the result of a person's faith in Jesus?

4. Do any of the negative qualities describe the way you relate to your ex (or to your spouse's ex)? What is the problem in relating this way?

5. What piece of Christ's "clothing" do you need to "put on" in your life now (see v. 12)?

   • How would doing this help your situation?

   • How would it help you regardless of how your ex responds?

   • How can others help you put it on?

REFERENCE NOTES

Colossians 3:1–14

3:4 This verse sums up the Christian's present reality and future hope. The Christian lives now through his or her union with Christ, but the full glory of that life will be manifested only when Christ himself returns.

3:5–14 The instructions in these verses are based on a common set of ethical teachings, used throughout the church to instruct converts in the way of Christ. The "put off" and "put on" metaphors may relate to the putting off and putting on of new clothes at a convert's baptism.

3:5 ***Put to death, therefore, what belongs to your earthly nature.*** While spiritually the believer has died and been raised to life with Christ (Col. 2:12,20; 3:1), he or she has to work out that reality on a daily basis (by continually choosing to turn away from attitudes and actions that reflect the old way of life).

3:8 ***you must rid yourselves of all such things.*** Immorality, greed, abusive talk (etc.) have no place in the life of a Christian. To repent means to consciously work at removing them from one's life.

3:12–14 Paul uses the image of putting on new clothes to show how true spirituality involves "wearing" the Christlike qualities of love, peace and thankfulness (Rom. 13:14).

3:12 ***compassion.*** This can be translated "a heart of pity." Such a person shows mercy to those who need it: the sick, the poor, the aged.

humility. A new virtue introduced by Christianity to the ancient world. This is an attitude based on the fact that all people are creatures created by (and for) God, so there is no room for arrogance.

3:13 ***Forgive as the Lord forgave you.*** The forgiveness of others by Christians is the best indication that they have grasped the reality of their need for the forgiveness of Christ (Matt. 6:14–15).

3:14 ***put on love.*** According to Jesus, to love God and others is the sum total of the meaning of the Law (Mark 12:30–31).

CARING TIME

Close by sharing prayer requests and by taking time to pray for one another. Ask for God's guidance and help in dealing with any difficult relationships in the coming week. Begin by having each group member answer the question:

"How can we help you in prayer this week?"

Then, move into prayer. At the close, join hands and repeat this prayer together:

*"Dear God, Grant us the serenity to accept the things
that we cannot control, the courage to change
the things we can, and the wisdom to
know the difference. Amen."*

LEADER:

If applicable, have the group use the extra space on this page for group prayer requests.

SESSION

5

The Stretching, Straining Family Ties

OBJECTIVES

To consider some common problems involved in the extended family relationships of blended families.

To share ways of dealing with the confusion sometimes created in this extensive family network.

To consider how David dealt with his strained relationship with King Saul.

THREE-PART AGENDA

ICE-BREAKER
15 Minutes

ISSUE / BIBLE STUDY
45 Minutes

CARING TIME
30 Minutes

OPTION: If you only have 60 minutes, divide this session into two sessions, with the Bible Study section for your next time together.

ICE-BREAKER

Pass out the Handout for this session or the course book to each person. Divide the group into subgroups of 4 to 6 to do the Ice-Breaker. (Photocopy pages 41 and 43 as needed.)

1. How many of your grandparents did you get to know as a child? What was one thing you really liked about your grandparents?

2. How many aunts and uncles did you have? Why was your favorite aunt or uncle your favorite?

3. At major holidays (like Thanksgiving and Christmas), did you travel to another family member's home, or did people come to your house? If you traveled, where did you go? Who was there? What traditions were part of that gathering?

INTRODUCTION TO THE ISSUE

LEADER:

• Summarize these remarks (in your own words) into a brief introduction (no longer than 5 minutes).

• Be careful not to read the entire presentation to the group.

• In your presentation cover the "Discuss the Issue" questions listed on Side One of the Handout.

Blended families do not consist of only the couple and their children. Blended families are made up of a wide network of people who are related to the children. If both parents have children from previous marriages, there are at least four sets of grandparents involved (not to mention countless aunts, uncles and cousins). And this is only the immediate family. If it is a challenge for first families to relate meaningfully to all the in-laws, it is even more of a challenge for blended families to stay connected.

In addition to the sheer number of people involved, it is important to remember the emotional atmosphere that surrounds blended families. Blended families, by their very definition, come into being as the result of loss. The fact that the blended family exists means that there was the death or divorce of a spouse. Either situation creates wounds of grief that affect the whole extended family. This emotional reality cannot help but color the way that the extended family relates to the blended family (and to you as the stepparent):

- As the new parent in the family, you may be favorably or unfavorably compared to the former spouse. In either case, this puts enormous pressure on you to "perform" in order to be (or remain) accepted.

- If the previous spouse has died, it is difficult to compete with the memory the deceased's parents have of that person. In their minds, he or she was the perfect father or mother against whom you are being compared.

- It is difficult to be placed in the role of the family's savior. If the former partner was seen as a "witch" or a "bum," you may be expected to bring the joy and happiness to your new spouse and stepchildren that they did not have in the previous relationship. It is tough to live up to such expectations. Furthermore, you cannot help but wonder if someday you may become "the bad person" in the eyes of your spouse's relatives!

It is hard to deal with the weight of expectations, stereotypes, unfair responses, caricatures, and unwarranted hostility that sometimes greets remarried spouses who are trying to forge a new and loving family. As in relating to stepchildren (or to a former spouse), a large dose of grace, creativity, patience and support is essential in forging ties with a new, extended family.

When this extensive combination of people (with its variety of emotional responses) is mixed together with events that focus on the children, the possibilities for problems seem endless! And such events abound. There are pleasant gatherings (such as recitals, birthdays, graduations, weddings and holiday celebrations). There are also difficult, painful times (such as illnesses, accidents and funerals). In either situation, tensions can erupt.

Cherie Burns, in her book *Stepmotherhood*, suggests some general principles to keep in mind in these types of situations:[1]

- Assume that everyone else is as uncertain and uncomfortable about the situation as you are. Realizing this may help you understand the social *faux pas* others make at times like this. What looks to you like an oversight (or neglect) may simply be confusion.

- Help others to be at ease by anticipating difficult situations and planning ahead. If your relationship with your spouse's ex is not a problem, assure people who are planning some event that involves both of you that you do get along all right. If the relationship is strained (but contact unavoidable), plan time afterward for you to unwind and process your feelings. Plan well ahead of time for holiday activities, so that everyone will not be left frazzled and frustrated.

- Stepchildren often dread holidays—they spend so much time traveling back and forth from one parent's home to another that it hardly seems worth the effort. Perhaps trading off holidays would be a better solution.

- Remember that you cannot control other people's attitudes toward you. Some in-laws may not be ready for friendly relationships with you, no matter who you are or what you do. While it is your responsibility to treat the members of your extended family with respect and consideration, it is not your responsibility to make them like you somehow.

- Probably the best way to break through the barriers that the extended family can put up is to demonstrate consistent integrity and love toward your spouse and stepchildren.

Relating to extended families is not all negative. This network of people can also be a great source of support, as the new stepparent navigates his or her way into the life of the family. For instance, a stepparent might be able to get valuable insights from the grandparents about ways to relate better to the child. A stepparent may also find that grandparents are eager to provide dependable, loving babysitting from time to time. A stepparent may discover that a new relative will become a good friend, eager to contribute to the stepparent's success as a spouse and parent. Over time, the new extended family (with all its uniqueness) can become your new family, which you come to love and cherish.

The Stretching, Straining Family Ties

ICE-BREAKER / Groups of 4 to 6 / 15 Minutes

1. How many of your grandparents did you get to know as a child? What was one thing you really liked about your grandparents?

2. How many aunts and uncles did you have? Why was your favorite aunt or uncle your favorite?

3. At major holidays (like Thanksgiving and Christmas), did you travel to another family member's home, or did people come to your house? If you traveled, where did you go? Who was there? What traditions were part of that gathering?

DISCUSS THE ISSUE / Same Groups / 20 Minutes

After a brief introduction by the leader, take turns sharing your responses to the following questions.

1. Name one specific issue that has caused tension in your life as a result of being part of an extended family.
   ❐ holidays and family gatherings
   ❐ unfair expectations
   ❐ stereotypes
   ❐ unwarranted hostility
   ❐ financial matters
   ❐ other:________________

2. How have you dealt with this issue in the past:
   - What have you learned about working through these tensions?
   - What logistical arrangements have helped?
   - What attitudes have helped?
   - How do you sustain those attitudes?

3. Are you concerned about an upcoming family event, or about a difficult relationship? Would you like to share it with the group?

INTRODUCTION TO THE BIBLE STUDY

David wrote this psalm while hiding from his enemy, King Saul. David had honored Saul as Israel's king; he had served him and respected him. But in return, David was accused of treason, and he was hated (and hunted) by Saul.

David's reaction to this unjust and threatening situation is instructive. Instead of seeking vengeance, he entrusted himself more and more to the care of God. He found his emotional safety in God, even as he found physical safety in the cave where he took refuge.

Listen while someone reads out loud Psalm 57. Then go around and take turns answering each of the questions that follow.

ICE-BREAKER FOR TWO-SESSION OPTION

If you are doing the Bible Study as a separate session, start off this session by dividing this group into subgroups of 4 to 6 and answering the following questions. Photocopy and give this to the group.

1. When you were a child, what was your favorite place to be?
- ❒ in your room
- ❒ in the yard
- ❒ at school
- ❒ at the beach
- ❒ in the woods
- ❒ at a friend's house
- ❒ in a room in the house (which one?)
- ❒ other:______________________

2. When times were hard as a child, where did you go to be alone and safe?
- ❒ your room
- ❒ outdoors (where?)
- ❒ in your clubhouse
- ❒ a secret place
- ❒ a private place in the house (behind the sofa?)
- ❒ other:______________________

3. Who (or what) would you take with you to this secret place?
- ❒ your dog
- ❒ a doll
- ❒ a book
- ❒ nobody (nothing)
- ❒ your best friend
- ❒ a sibling
- ❒ other:______________

4. Where do you go now, when you need a "safe place" to get away from the pressure?

SESSION FIVE BIBLE STUDY

57 ***Have mercy on me, O God, have mercy on me,***
for in you my soul takes refuge.
I will take refuge in the shadow of your wings
until the disaster has passed.
2 I cry out to God Most High,
to God, who fulfills his purpose for me.
3 He sends from heaven and saves me,
rebuking those who hotly pursue me;
God sends his love and his faithfulness.
4 I am in the midst of lions;
I lie among ravenous beasts—
men whose teeth are spears and arrows,
whose tongues are sharp swords.
5 Be exalted, O God, above the heavens;
let your glory be over all the earth.
6 They spread a net for my feet—
I was bowed down in distress.
They dug a pit in my path—
but they have fallen into it themselves.
7 My heart is steadfast, O God,
my heart is steadfast;
I will sing and make music.
8 Awake, my soul!
Awake, harp and lyre!
9 I will praise you, O Lord, among the nations;
I will sing of you among the peoples.
10 For great is your love, reaching to the heavens;
your faithfulness reaches to the skies.
11 Be exalted, O God, above the heavens;
let your glory be over all the earth.

Psalm 57

1. Looking at this Psalm, how do you think David's relationship with God helped him during the hard times?

2. Which phrases in this Psalm express how you've felt about your spouse's extended family?

3. At those times when relatives from your extended family seem like "lions and ravenous beasts" (that are threatening to devour you), how can God help you?
   - ❒ by reminding me of his unconditional love for me
   - ❒ by protecting me
   - ❒ by "rebuking those who hotly pursue me" (v. 3)
   - ❒ other:____________________________________

REFERENCE NOTES

Psalm 57

57:1 ***in you my soul takes refuge.*** Given the physical danger that David was in, it appeared that his only refuge was the cave. In fact, his real trust was in God.

wings. The believer's security in God is sometimes compared to a nestling bird, sheltered by its mother's wings to protect it during a storm (Ruth 2:12; Psalm 61:4; Matthew 23:37).

57:2 ***God Most High.***This title for God is seldom found outside of the Psalms. The early Canaanites used it as the common title for their supreme being. The patriarch Abraham claimed it for the Lord (Gen. 14:18). The Most High God is the One who has pledged himself to protect and shelter David from harm. As verse 3 indicates, the emphasis on God's transcendence in this title does not make God remote. God is a very present help for those who call upon him.

57:4 ***lions ... beasts.*** Comparing one's enemies to ferocious animals was common. It is a metaphor that highlights their evil intentions. See also Psalm 22:12-13.

57:5 This verse is the refrain of the psalm. See also verse 11. It stresses that whether in hardship (vv. 1–4) or deliverance (vv. 6–10), what is ultimately important is that God's glory be made evident to all.

57:8 David's joy is so great that he wants to sing loudly enough to wake up the dawn.

57:9 David's joy involves sharing the good news of God's deliverance with anyone who will listen! In Romans 15:9, Paul uses these verses as a prophecy of the way the Gospel will be proclaimed to all the world by those who are enthralled with its message of God's goodness.

57:10–11 As the psalm comes to a close, three primary qualities of God are emphasized.

57:10 ***love.*** In order to stress that this is a love which can be counted upon, some versions translate this word as "steadfast love."

faithfulness. Though all else may be in chaos, one can count on God to keep his promises. Through his rescue, David has experienced both the love and the dependability of God.

57:11 ***glory.*** This word is most often used to describe God's tremendous influence and power. David celebrates the fact that the glory of God is not restricted to heaven, but is evidenced throughout the earth wherever his love and faithfulness are displayed.

CARING TIME

Take time now to share any personal prayer requests. This meeting may have brought up some painful situations with our extended families. Use this time to pray for one another, in light of the feelings that have been shared. Go around the group and have each person pray for the person on their left. Let group members know that there is no presssure to pray out loud. They can pray silently if that is their preference. Start with this sentence:

"Dear God, please help ______________________
as he or she faces ______________________."

When each person has had a turn, join hands and thank God that he loves us more than we can know and promises to meet our every need.

LEADER:

If applicable, have the group use the extra space on this page for group prayer requests.

SESSION

6

Nurturing the Marriage

OBJECTIVES

To think about ways to strengthen the bond between husband and wife in a blended family.

To explore how to nurture a marriage in which there are stepchildren.

To examine a passage from the Song of Songs about intimacy and love.

THREE-PART AGENDA

ICE-BREAKER
15 Minutes

ISSUE / BIBLE STUDY
45 Minutes

CARING TIME
30 Minutes

OPTION: If you only have 60 minutes, divide this session into two sessions, with the Bible Study section for your next time together.

ICE-BREAKER

Pass out the Handout for this session or the course book to each person. Divide the group into subgroups of 4 to 6 to do the Ice-Breaker. (Photocopy pages 49 and 51 as needed.)

The REAL Me. In the following categories, check the item you would pick and place an *"X"* beside the item you think your spouse would pick.

1. Finding a movie to watch on a quiet evening:
______ an adventure film like *Indiana Jones*
______ a love story like *You've Got Mail*
______ a sci-fi film like *Star Wars: The Phantom Menace*
______ a comedy like *Father of the Bride*
______ a classic film like *Gone With the Wind*

2. Adding to your bedroom:
______ a waterbed
______ a private hot tub
______ built-in entertainment center
______ an exercise machine
______ a private bathroom
______ new wallpaper

3. Finding a place to go on a date:
______ a quiet moonlit walk
______ dancing
______ dinner in an elegant restaurant
______ bowling
______ a play
______ a sports event

INTRODUCTION TO THE ISSUE

LEADER:

• Summarize these remarks (in your own words) into a brief introduction (no longer than 5 minutes).

• Be careful not to read the entire presentation to the group.

• In your presentation cover the "Discuss the Issue" questions listed on Side One of the Handout.

When people remarry, they do so with the hope of establishing a loving, nurturing union. The fact that they have been married before often provides them with maturity and self-understanding that they did not have when they were married the first time. Furthermore, their views of marriage are likely to be far more realistic and honest. In other words, such a couple has the potential to form a really good marriage.

However, this will not happen automatically or without work. In particular, the realities of stepparenting have to be faced squarely. These complexities must not be allowed to take up the time remarried couples need to nurture their new relationship.

In a remarriage, while it is necessary to be sensitive to the needs of the children, it is crucial that a couple make their own relationship primary. If this bond is not developed, the family has little hope of surviving as a unit. The divorce rate for second marriages is higher (60%) than for first marriages (50%). The majority of second marriages that fail do so within the first three years. Even if there is no divorce, there may be emotional fragmentation and isolation of the family members from one another.

The result can be what family counselors call a relationship triangle. This is the process by which two people in a family draw together, while distancing a third member. This is seen when a mother comforts a child after an unreasonable outburst by a father, or when two siblings unite against a third who is being unfair. In healthy families, these triangles constantly shift (depending on the circumstances). In blended families, however, the triangles become fixed. Since the original bond between parent and child is more established than the bond between the new spouses, a triangle can be set up where it is *always* mother and son against the stepfather. Such a triangle can express itself in various ways. These include consistently putting the needs of the child before those of the spouse, failing to protect the privacy of the marriage because of the fear of alienating the child, or not supporting a stepparent's attempts at reasonable discipline.

The real need of children (especially those from divorced homes) is to see a model of a loving man and woman working together to form a family. The primary purpose of remarriage is not to provide another parent for the children. It is to become companions to one another for, "it is not good that the man (or woman) be alone" (Gen. 2:18). There is great pain for everyone when first marriages are terminated. Remarriage can offer a sign of God's grace, by providing another opportunity for the intimacy and emotional security that marriage was designed to provide. As couples embrace this new opportunity (doing all they can to nurture it), one of the overlooked benefits of blended families begins to occur: The children have the chance to see a role model of the beauty, importance and joy of marriage.

There are many ways for couples with children to nurture this type of marriage. Some suggestions include:

- Plan and guard regular time for you and your spouse alone. Dates, day trips and vacations alone are valuable. Kids can be included at other times, but make sure there is time set aside for just the two of you.

- Some single parents have adopted patterns of living that need to be altered when they marry. While closing and locking the bedroom door may make you feel that you are rejecting your child (who was such a good friend to you during your time of singleness), this is an important sign to your spouse that he or she comes first.

- Set time aside regularly (especially in the beginning) to evaluate how things are going. Flexibility is essential, since there are no standardized rules that can be applied to the variety of needs and demands upon a blended family. Keep the lines of communication open about money, logistical arrangements and relationships with the extended family.

- A partner who inherits a blended family is often hesitant to express his or her needs, frustrations and fears. There are various reasons for this: The desire to demonstrate to the spouse what a good parent he or she can be (despite not having any children of one's own), not wanting to upset the spouse, or because of the refusal to honestly face one's limits. Thus, it is important to create opportunities when such honest sharing can take place. Too often, these feelings are suppressed until a time of crisis (then it is impossible to deal with them constructively).

- Remember that you married each other because you were in love and wanted to be close to each other. Stepparents can get so busy with all the details of life that this fact is forgotten. Think of ways that you can express love to one another, even in the midst of hectic times.

- If you find yourselves stuck or in strong disagreement over certain family issues, you will probably find it helpful to get outside, professional input. Visit a family counselor, join a support group, or make an appointment with your priest or minister. A counselor's role is not to decide which of you is right. Rather it is to help you come to grips with your problem in such a way that you both can feel positive about its solution. Furthermore, counseling can help you see patterns in your life and marriage that both of you are blind to on your own. Don't be afraid to seek help.[2]

Nurturing your marriage will be well worth the time and effort. Your relationship will certainly grow, and your children will benefit as they see a role model of what a good marriage is all about.

Nurturing the Marriage

ICE-BREAKER / Groups of 4 to 6 / 15 Minutes

The REAL Me. In the following categories, check the item you would pick and place an *"X"* beside the item you think your spouse would pick.

1. Finding a movie to watch on a quiet evening:
______ an adventure film like *Indiana Jones*
______ a love story like *You've Got Mail*
______ a sci-fi film like *Star Wars: The Phantom Menace*
______ a comedy like *Father of the Bride*
______ a classic film like *Gone With the Wind*

2. Adding to your bedroom:
______ a waterbed
______ a private hot tub
______ built-in entertainment center
______ an exercise machine
______ a private bathroom
______ new wallpaper

3. Finding a place to go on a date:
______ a quiet moonlit walk
______ dancing
______ dinner in an elegant restaurant
______ bowling
______ a play
______ a sports event

DISCUSS THE ISSUE / Same Groups / 20 Minutes

After a brief introduction by the leader, take turns sharing your responses to the following questions.

1. What positive ideas about love and marriage will your children (and/or stepchildren) receive from watching your marriage now?

2. Of the suggestions given in the introduction for nurturing your relationship with one another, which one do you think your spouse is most excited about?

3. What is one way you would like to nurture your relationship as the primary bond in your family?
❒ plan a regular date time
❒ set time aside for evaluation
❒ share honestly and openly
❒ seek outside help, such as support or family counseling
❒ other:____

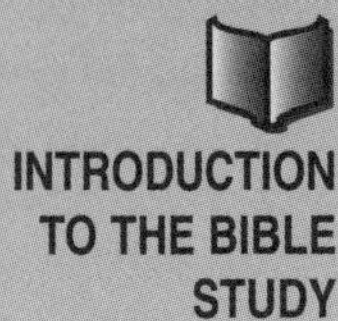

INTRODUCTION TO THE BIBLE STUDY

The Song of Songs is a celebration of love between a man and a woman which is akin to God's love for his people. Readers are sometimes surprised to find an explicit love song in the Bible. While many of the images used are quite culture-bound, it is clear that this unidentified couple thoroughly enjoyed each other, and they made sure each other knew it! For this reason, the Song of Songs can become a reminder to us of the importance of nurturing and celebrating our love for our spouses.

Listen while someone reads out loud this Scripture passage from Song of Songs. Then go around and take turns answering the questions that follow.

ICE-BREAKER FOR TWO-SESSION OPTION

If you are doing the Bible Study as a separate session, start off this session by dividing this group into subgroups of 4 to 6 and answering the following questions. Photocopy and give this to the group.

1. Think back to your first elementary school sweetheart. What do you remember about him or her? About your "romance"?

2. What was "romance" like for you in high school?
❒ Everything's coming up roses.
❒ Romance? You've got to be kidding!
❒ Well, there was this one guy/girl ...
❒ Some dates but no fireworks.
❒ I was in love but he/she wasn't.
❒ Who had time?

3. What do you remember about the first time you met your spouse? What struck you about him or her?
❒ striking good looks
❒ dashing wit
❒ brilliant intellect
❒ shared values
❒ money (or lack of it)
❒ personality
❒ other:____________________________________

SESSION SIX BIBLE STUDY

Lover

14My dove in the clefts of the rock,
in the hiding places on the mountainside,
show me your face.
let me hear your voice;
for your voice is sweet,
and your face is lovely.
15Catch for us the foxes,
the little foxes
that ruin the vineyards,
our vineyards that are in bloom.

Beloved

16My lover is mine and I am his;
he browses among the lilies.
17Until the day breaks
and the shadows flee,
turn, my lover,
and be like a gazelle
or like a young stag
on the rugged hills.

Song of Songs 2:14–17

1. In these verses, the couple enjoys a secret rendezvous. How does the beloved's comment (in the first part of verse 16) set the context for that enjoyment?

2. What are the most important components of genuine intimacy in marriage?
❐ enjoying the same activities
❐ sharing all our thoughts with one another
❐ agreeing on important issues
❐ having sex together
❐ being best friends to one another
❐ sharing the same spirituality
❐ other:______________________________

3. In the same way that a vinedresser has to guard against animals who will destroy the vineyard, so the man is aware that "little foxes" can ruin love (v. 15). What "little foxes" in blended family life have the potential to ruin love? How can you restrict their influence?

REFERENCE NOTES

Song of Songs 2:14–17

Summary. Interpretations of this ancient book vary widely. Some view it as a celebration of King Solomon's love for his bride. Others see it as an allegory depicting Christ's love for his bride, the Church. This latter view probably emerged as Christians developed more puritan attitudes about sex. However, God does not seem to share the reservations some of his people have about sex. This book serves as a reminder to us that sex and love is a delicious gift which God has given people to enjoy within marriage. In that light, it is perhaps best to view this poem as a celebration of romantic love at its best.

2:14 ***dove in the cleft of the rock.*** Rock pigeons make their homes in cliffs, safe from intruders. So the man and the woman seek a hidden place to be together.

2:15 ***the little foxes.*** These could be foxes or jackals. Both destroyed vineyards and had to be guarded against. This verse may express the man's desire to remove all hindrances to their relationship.

2:16 ***My lover is mine and I am his.*** An expression of the emotional and sexual unity of love. They are mutually giving and receiving from each other, freely choosing to belong to one another in fidelity.

he browses among the lilies. The woman is *not* watching the man strolling through a garden. This is another sexual metaphor: She is the garden—the flower whose beauty and softness he takes time throughout the night to enjoy thoroughly.

turn ... be like a gazelle. The man cannot safely stay, so the woman compares him to a deer feeding in the safety of night (but needing to run away when dawn breaks).

CARING TIME

Take time now to share any concerns and pray for one another. Have each group member answer the question:

"How can we help you in prayer this week?"

Then, move into prayer. At the close, join hands and pray this prayer together.

"Dear God, Thank you for the gift of love
that you have given to each couple here.
Help us all to nurture our marriages and
find the right path to true intimacy—
an intimacy that includes sexuality,
spirituality, and the open sharing
of feelings. Amen."

LEADER:

If applicable, have the group use the extra space on this page for group prayer requests.

SESSION

7

Finding Inner Strength

OBJECTIVES

To consider how we can develop inner resources to cope with family pressure.

To examine a passage from John about who Jesus is and what he provides for us.

To plan the next step for us personally and as a group.

THREE-PART AGENDA

ICE-BREAKER
15 Minutes

ISSUE / BIBLE STUDY
45 Minutes

CARING TIME
30 Minutes

NOTE: The agenda is reversed and there is no two-session option.

ICE-BREAKER

We recommend that you use the Ice-Breaker at the close of this session—as part of the Evaluation / Caring Time. This affirmation exercise is on the back of the Handout. (Photocopy pages 57 and 59 as needed.)

NOTE: Ice-Breaker goes last with Evaluation / Caring Time.

And the Award Goes To ... You have had a chance to observe the gifts and talents of the members of your group. Now, you will have a chance to pass out some much deserved praise for the contribution that each member of the group has made to your life. Read out loud the first award. Then, let everyone nominate the person they feel is the most deserving for that award. Then read the next award, etc., through the list. Have fun!

SPARK PLUG AWARD: The person who ignited the group.

DEAR ABBY AWARD: The person who cared enough to listen.

WINNIE THE POOH AWARD: The warm, caring person when someone needed a hug.

OPRAH AWARD: The person who asked fun questions that got us to talk.

TED KOPPEL AWARD: The person who asked the heavy questions that made us think.

more ⟶

KING ARTHUR AWARD: The knight in shining armor who saved damsels in distress.

PINK PANTHER AWARD: The detective who made us deal with Scripture.

TRAFFIC COP AWARD: The person who went out of their way to keep order in the meetings

SERENDIPITY CROWN: The person who grew the most spiritually during the course (in your estimation).

INTRODUCTION TO THE ISSUE

LEADER:

• Summarize these remarks (in your own words) into a brief introduction (no longer than 5 minutes).

• Be careful not to read the entire presentation to the group.

• In your presentation cover the "Discuss the Issue" questions listed on Side One of the Handout.

While a support system (made up of an understanding spouse and other warm, open people) is important for a stepparent, there is also the need for inner spiritual resources. Each person needs spiritual strength that is not dependent on any other person. Successful living in a blended family requires qualities that can only be developed and sustained on a spiritual basis.

For example, stepparenting requires that we:

- Learn to accept and enjoy ourselves for who we are, independent of negative or positive input that we are getting from others.
- Discern between real guilt (that we must deal with) and false guilt (that others try to put on us).
- Learn patterns of honest, open relationships (rather than relying on manipulative tactics).
- Not be fearful in the face of so many factors which affect us, over which we have no control.
- Accept others as they are (instead of trying to force them to fit with our agenda).
- Cultivate habits of forgiveness and grace (rather than resentment and bitterness).
- Appreciate the good gifts in our life, even during hard times.
- Live in love toward others who actively dislike us.
- Have a primary relationship with God (rather than expecting our spouse to fulfill our deepest needs).

What a list! Who can hope to be this sort of person on his or her own? Of course, this list of inner qualities is merely suggestive, not absolute. It does, however, illustrate how needy we are for spiritual resources. Each of the qualities above is directly related to the spiritual life.

Sometimes, however, we search for these qualities in the wrong places. We seek peace, security and meaning in life by turning to what the world has to offer—things such as drugs, alcohol, food, entertainment, excessive work and activities, etc. We may blame other people for our problems, feeling that our only hope is to change relationships once again. Eventually, we may assume that there is no hope, and resign ourselves to a life of quiet, depressed resignation.

There is a more positive way to find peace, security, and meaning amidst the pressures of blended family life. This is the path of spiritual commitment. Those who open themselves up to the spiritual develop a pattern of living that changes the way they view life in general. They are no longer struggling in a vain attempt to control everything (nor are they mired in despair because they realize they can't). Rather, they are learning to accept life as it comes, with the deep confidence that they are loved and valued by God (whom they trust with those areas of life that are uncontrollable).

Spiritual growth involves, first of all, a decision to place oneself under God's authority and care. In the New Testament, there are two words that describe how to do this. These words are *repentance* and *faith.* Repentance is the act of deciding to turn from ways of living that are opposed to God's ways. It is the decision to turn to God. Faith is the act of reaching out in trust to Jesus, asking him to bring us to God (while believing that by his death and resurrection, he opened the way back to God for all people).

The spiritual life, then, becomes an ongoing commitment. The Bible refers to it as "walking in the Spirit," "putting on Christ," or "following Jesus." All of these terms imply a progressive, continuous way of life. All branches of the Christian faith emphasize that such a way of life needs to be nurtured through spiritual disciplines (like Bible reading and reflection, prayer, loving service and corporate worship). Furthermore, one's life in Christ is not strictly a private affair. It involves becoming part of the community of faith. The shared experience of faith enables the whole community to grow in qualities such as peace, love, endurance and forgiveness.

Of course, developing these inner spiritual qualities will not automatically result in a stress-free blended family life. Some people approach Christ as though he were the genie in Aladdin's lamp: "If we curry favor with him, he will grant us our wishes." But there is no such lamp! Christians are not automatically freed from problems. In Christ, however, we find strength to respond to problems with grace and love. Marriage into a blended family may be the most intense course you will ever take concerning the real meaning of spiritual life!

SESSION SEVEN HANDOUT: Blended Families

Finding Inner Strength

DISCUSS THE ISSUE (Groups of 4 to 6 / 20 Min.)

1. Of the spiritual qualities presented in the Introduction, which one strikes you as the one you would like to nourish in your life right now? How has being part of a blended family contributed to your awareness of this need?

2. What is one positive step you can take to nurture the spiritual core of your life?
   - ❒ Set aside some quiet time a few days a week to pray and read the Bible.
   - ❒ Commit my life to Christ.
   - ❒ Attend a church and learn to worship God.
   - ❒ Start a journal to record my thoughts, prayers, concerns and insights.
   - ❒ Get involved with a group that takes spirituality seriously, and try to learn more from other people's experiences.
   - ❒ other:____

RESPOND TO THE BIBLE STUDY (Same Groups / 20 Min.)

47 I tell you the truth, he who believes has everlasting life. 48 I am the bread of life. 49 Your fore-
fathers ate the manna in the desert, yet they died. 50 But here is the bread that comes down
from heaven, which a man may eat and not die. 51 I am the living bread that came down from
heaven. If anyone eats of this bread, he will live forever. This bread is my flesh, which I will give for the life of the world."

John 6:47–51

1. What does the image of bread convey? What does this image say about who Jesus is, and how he relates to us?

2. On a scale of 1 (distant) to 10 (very close), how would you describe your relationship with Jesus at this time?

3. To benefit from bread, we must eat it. What is your next step in developing your relationship with Jesus?

INTRODUCTION TO THE BIBLE STUDY

Jesus often utilized word-pictures (images, metaphors) to speak about spiritual realities. In this passage from John's Gospel, he uses the image of bread to communicate the central role that he plays in meeting the deep inner needs we all have for nurture, meaning and hope.

In this powerful passage, Jesus reveals to us that he is bread for the hungry. As such, he invites us to come and know him—that we might be full, enlightened and directed. The spiritual needs unmasked by our lives in a blended family are the same needs he has come to meet.

Listen carefully, while someone reads out loud this Scripture passage from John. Then go around and take turns answering the questions that follow.

REFERENCE NOTES

John 6:47–51

6:47 ***I tell you the truth.*** This phrase is used throughout the Gospel whenever John wants to introduce a critical statement. Here, Jesus sums up (in a single promise) all he has said in the preceding verses: Whoever believes in him has life.

6:48 ***I am the bread of life.*** This is the first of seven sayings in John's Gospel that highlight Jesus' identity and mission by use of a metaphor. Bread was the staple food for the people, sometimes the only food they had available. Its availability was essential to life. By comparing himself to bread, Jesus is saying that just as bread nourishes them with physical life, so he is the source of spiritual life for those who come to him (see also John 3:15).

6:49 ***Your forefathers ate ... yet they died.*** Jesus had just performed the miracle of feeding five thousand people with five small loaves of bread and two small fish. The intent of this miracle was to show that one greater than Moses was on the scene (and ought to be listened to). Jesus explains that the bread he provides is superior to the manna provided to their forefathers in the desert. Whereas those who literally ate the manna eventually died, whoever spiritually feeds on "the bread that comes down from heaven" will live forever.

6:51 ***This bread is my flesh.*** Since this passage is similar to those in the Last Supper accounts (Matt. 26:26,28; Mark 14:22,24; Luke 22:19,20), John appears to be using this discussion about Jesus as a way of instructing his readers about the real purpose of the Lord's Supper.

Finding Inner Strength

ICE-BREAKER / All Together / 45 Minutes (Total)

And the Award Goes To ... You have had a chance to observe the gifts and talents of the members of your group. Now, you will have a chance to pass out some much deserved praise for the contribution that each member of the group has made to your life. Read out loud the first award. Then, let everyone nominate the person they feel is the most deserving for that award. Then read the next award, etc., through the list. Have fun!

SPARK PLUG AWARD: The person who ignited the group.

DEAR ABBY AWARD: The person who cared enough to listen.

WINNIE THE POOH AWARD: The warm, caring person when someone needed a hug.

OPRAH AWARD: The person who asked fun questions that got us to talk.

TED KOPPEL AWARD: The person who asked the heavy questions that made us think.

KING ARTHUR AWARD: The knight in shining armor who saved damsels in distress.

PINK PANTHER AWARD: The detective who made us deal with Scripture.

TRAFFIC COP AWARD: The person who went out of their way to keep order in the meetings.

SERENDIPITY CROWN: The person who grew the most spiritually during the course (in your estimation).

EVALUATION / CARING TIME / 30 Minutes

Take a few minutes to review your experience and reflect. Go around on each question and share your answers. When you have finished with the questions, take time to share prayer requests and close in prayer.

1. When you first started this course, how were you feeling?
2. How did you feel about opening up and sharing yourself with this group?
3. What was one of the most significant things you learned?
4. What was the high point in this course for you?
5. What did you appreciate most about the group?

CONTINUATION

Do you want to continue as a group? If so, what do you need to improve? Finish the sentence:

"If I were to suggest one thing we could work on as a group, it would be ... "

MAKE A COVENANT

A covenant is a promise made to each other in the presence of God. Its purpose is to indicate your intention to make yourselves available to one another for the fulfillment of the purposes you share. In a spirit of prayer, work your way through the following sentences, trying to reach an agreement on each statement pertaining to your ongoing life together. Write out your covenant like a contract, stating your purpose, goals, and the ground rules for your group.

1. The purpose of our group will be:

2. Our goals will be:

3. We will meet for _____weeks, after which we will decide if we wish to continue as a group.

4. We will meet from _____ to ______ and we will strive to start on time and end on time.

5. We will meet at ____________________ (place) or we will rotate from house to house.

6. We will agree to the following ground rules for our group (check):

- ❒ PRIORITY: While you are in the course, you give the group meetings priority.
- ❒ PARTICIPATION: Everyone participates and no one dominates.
- ❒ RESPECT: Everyone is given the right to their own opinion, and all questions are encouraged and respected.
- ❒ CONFIDENTIALITY: Anything that is said in the meeting is never repeated outside the meeting.
- ❒ EMPTY CHAIR: The group stays open to new people at every meeting, as long as they understand the ground rules.

- ❒ SUPPORT: Permission is given to call upon each other in time of need at any time.
- ❒ ACCOUNTABILITY: We agree to let the members of the group hold us accountable to the commitments which each of us make in whatever loving ways we decide upon.
- ❒ ADVICE-GIVING: Unsolicited advice is not allowed.
- ❒ MISSION: We agree to do everything in our power to start a new group as our mission.

CURRICULUM AND OTHER FELT NEED GROUP COURSES

Other FELT NEED GROUP COURSES in this series are listed below. For more information about other group resources and possible direction, please contact your small group coordinator or SERENDIPITY at 1-800-525-9563 or visit us at: www.serendipityhouse.com.

12 STEPS: The Path to Wholeness

HEALTHY RELATIONSHIPS: Living Within Defined Boundaries

DEALING WITH GRIEF AND LOSS: Hope in the Midst of Pain

PARENTING ADOLESCENTS: Easing the Way to Adulthood

MARRIAGE ENRICHMENT: Making a Good Marriage Better

STRESS MANAGEMENT: Finding the Balance

DIVORCE RECOVERY: Picking Up the Pieces

RESOURCES FOR FURTHER STUDY

The *Serendipity Bible for Groups* contains a number of Questionnaire Bible Studies. Generally there is no "right" answer to these questions. The answers reflect your understanding and your experience. The name for this sort of small group exercise is relational Bible study, since the focus is more on the people in the group than on delving deeply into the text. You can do more rigorous Bible study by using the questions in the margin of the *Serendipity Bible for Groups.*

What follows are 14 suggested studies—seven from the Old Testament and seven from the New Testament. While these questionnaire studies do not always focus directly on blended families, they all discuss some aspect of the topic. These studies are listed in the order in which they occur in the Bible, not in the order in which you will necessarily want to study them.

Studies From the Old Testament

1. Adam and Eve (Genesis 2:4–25)
Explore the nature of the marriage relationship.

2. The Tower of Babel (Genesis 11:1–9)
Explore the power of communication and the impact of change.

3. The Call of Abram (Genesis 11:27–12:7)
Explore the need for faith in the journey of life.

4. Joseph Makes Himself Known (Genesis 45:1–28)
Explore the role of forgiveness in dealing with difficult relationships.

5. Moses and the Burning Bush (Exodus 3:1–22)
Explore the relationship of fear versus faith in facing hard times.

6. David and Goliath (1 Samuel 17:12–50)
Explore how to face issues that seem overwhelming.

7. Nathan Rebukes David (2 Samuel 12:1–14)
Explore the importance of learning from mistakes.

Studies From the New Testament

1. Jesus Walks on Water (Matthew 14:22–33)
   Explore how difficult circumstances can strengthen faith.

2. The Parable of the Unmerciful Servant (Matthew 18:21–35)
   Explore how to develop a forgiving attitude toward others.

3. The Parable of the Prodigal Son (Luke 15:11–32)
   Explore the challenges of parenting difficult children.

4. The Parable of the Pharisee and the Tax Collector (Luke 18:9–14)
   Explore the importance of a proper self-image.

5. Peter Disowns Jesus (Luke 22:54–62)
   Explore how to deal with failure.

6. Jesus Talks With a Samaritan Woman (John 4:7–30)
   Explore how Jesus can help us through the pressures and stress of everyday life.

7. Jesus Washes the Disciples' Feet (John 13:1–17)
   Explore what it means to care for others through serving.

ENDNOTES:

[1]Cherie Burns, *Stepmotherhood* (Times Books, 1986).
[2]Barbara Kantrowitz and Pat Wingert, *Step by Step,* Newsw
21st Century Family, Winter/Spring, 1990.

PERSONAL NOTES